PURE DELICIOUS *Love*

C A WILLIAMS

AuthorHouse™ UK
1663 Liberty Drive
Bloomington, IN 47403 USA
www.authorhouse.co.uk
Phone: 0800.197.4150

Published by AuthorHouse 02/06/2019

ISBN: 978-1-7283-8428-3 (sc)
ISBN: 978-1-7283-8427-6 (e)

Print information available on the last page.

Any people depicted in stock imagery provided by Getty Images are models, and such images are being used for illustrative purposes only. Certain stock imagery © Getty Images.

This book is printed on acid-free paper.

author**HOUSE**®

This book was inspired by my awesome son Drew, my beautiful mother Sereta and all my present family members and all future family members.

God's Love

God's love is as big as the sky
And flows through me and you
So when you're feeling sad
He knows just what to do
He kisses you with a rainbow
And fills your heart with joy
With mountain cups of so much love
Bigger and brighter than any toy

Endless Possibilities

Anything is possible
Just let God be your guide
Trust in he and you will see
Before your very eyes
He'll walk with you and hold your hand
To light you on your way
So step in the light and colours so bright
Because God is here to stay

You Are Safe

You are safe my child
In God's loving arms
Like a rainbow surrounding you
With all it's charms
When you breathe in and out
The magic flows
Like a fountain of love
That grows and grows

Smile and Connect

God is love and that is all
That can make you feel over 10 feet tall
So let it flow from me to you
Each other revealed through and through
Be still and smile as we connect
To love in it's fullest; 'God's Internet'

God's light

You are the light that God sends through
Into your life and all you do
To make sure that we know our way
And everything we hear and say
Is filled with goodness and nothing more
Than fountains of love for all to adore

God's Secret

You can have it all
It's all inside of you
Just ask very simply
For either one or two
The knowing is the answer
To what you know you want
And always add a thank you
To seal, 'God's Loving Grant'

Lullaby

Sleep my dear with God's love
Surrounding you like God's angels from above
Tired now so close your eyes
And taste the delight of a thousand skies
If you awake before daylight
Just to wet your appetite
Take a peak of God's true love
Covering you like a wave from above

A Rainbow's Eyes

When you look into a rainbow
Always remember 'He'
Because the colours of a rainbow
Will show you how to be free
Your eyes mirror the colours of light
That flow from God to you
So begin to know and your love will flow
With perfect synchronicity

Divine Love

Take a deep breath and count to ten
And then you will see God's love again and again
There is no fear when you trust in 'He'
There are only ways, to be free
So look for him in every way
For he is here and never strays
For you are his and will always be
His truest form of divinity

Love Is Giving

When people are not nice to you
Remember this is true
That always deep inside of them
They feel so sad and blue
So radiate your astounding love
So they can feel it too
And know that love is endless
When it flows from the God within you

True Love

He loves you, he loves you, he loves you
How is it that you don't see
That to give you the world is just a clue
Of his endless love to thee
You are his precious creation
And he will always be
Eternally grateful for every day
That you walk through this world knowing 'He'

You Are The key

It is all within you
You feel that this is true
It's all as big as the ocean
With vastness that's oh so blue
So try and try to believe
And then you will truly know
That all you ever wished for
Will magically overflow

A Parent's Love

Your mother is here to watch over you
And love you when you're down
Your father is here to be strong for you
Even when he's not around
The light you see in the daytime
Is God walking with you all the way
And the twinkling stars at night time
Are God's blessings as a Universal Spray

Be Happy

Know that when you smile
God is always there
As a smile is his biggest way
To show you how much he cares
Happiness is love
So plainly to be seen
So smile and smile and smile again
Show everyone your magnificent sheen

You Are Loved

When you're out and about
And having fun
And someone makes you feel like
'They're the only one'
Remember that God's love for you
can shatter any fear
So live with the Universal love that
can make any fog become clear

Love's Journey

I searched for the answer to my prayers
And dared to look where no one dared
And then the answer came to me
Without even looking with my eyes to see
That his endless love is everywhere
And he answers every single prayer
Through streams and cities it flows like a light
That shines like a star on the darkest night

Soul Mates

The one you love is yours
It has always been this way
Before your birth it's decided
That you both would meet one day

So love each other dearly
And cherish the time you share
And love will grow to knowing
Your soul mate truly cares

It Is Yours

Let go and just let it flow
Just close your eyes and be free
Then smile and know it is given
Before you count to three

For God is always listening
To everything you say
For like a mother, 'He' knows
What you want before you pray

God Is You

When you cry he cries too
So realise that this is true
You are he and he is you
We are all connected
Through and through

A Baby's Knowledge

A baby is pure spirit
Still with it's heavenly bond
It's knowledge is fantastic
As God and baby still correspond

They know about the universe
And universes beyond
So see them for their purity
To really truly bond

A Child's Truth

When a child is growing
Listen to all they say
'Cause they can really teach you
What God would truly say

For they are so pure in spirit
And powerful and true
They know the hidden secrets
That God would speak to you

God's Flow

When everything is flowing
Don't question anything
For this is the greatest time
For you to truly sing

For like a dolphin goes
With the flow of the ocean's waves
You're flowing with the universe
Just let go, smile and be brave

Colourful

Whatever we look like
We are everyone the same
If only you could see into
God's bigger universal game

For beyond what our eyes see
The invisible is true
In each of us lies every colour
Like a rainbow through and through

Be Still

Be quiet, be still and listen
For the answer is in you
To each and every duty
You have for God to do

For God truly speaks through you
Just listen carefully
Then everything is answered
You are given every possibility

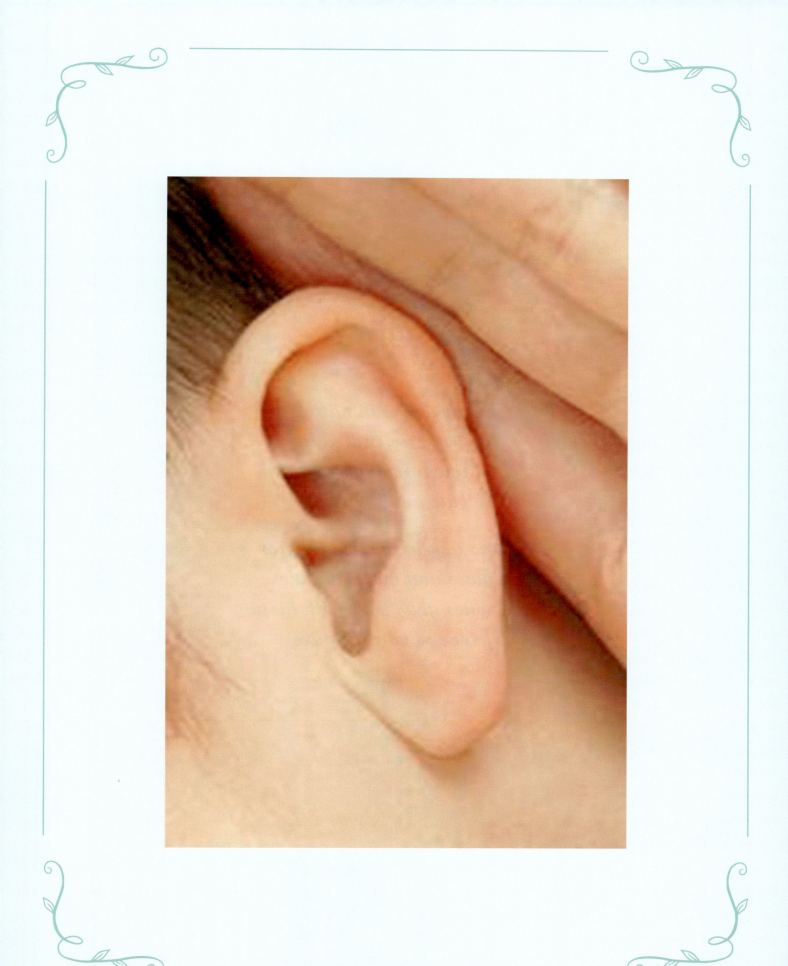

Nature

The answer is in nature
It speaks so endlessly
Just like a loving parent
So true and lovingly

It hugs you in the down times
And gives you more and more
And strokes your soul with kisses
Of love so true an pure

The Ultimate Father

Everywhere you walk
Know that 'He' is there
To light the way before you
And love you everywhere

You are his love; his love child
Who brings God so much peace
He is the ultimate father
His love will never cease

Reflection

When you look into the mirror
Tell me what you see
Look deep into your eyes
And know that, that is 'He'

For in this knowledge you open
The beauty that is within
Because we are pure oneness
The original truth, free of sin

He Is There

Feel God flow right through you
It'll make you feel so good
He is there before you feel him
He'll never be your judge

He's been there before you were
Feeding you with his love
Fulfilling your every appitete
For goodness from Angels above

Your Truth

People may look at you and stare
And say 'what she's done with her hair'
But just remember all ideas
Come from a place with no fear
So stand up tall and proud with those
Whom God loves for, he has no foes

Daily Blessings

Each day is a blessing
From God's sweet love
Sent here with whispers
From the Angels above

So cherish each moment
With loving care
To prove to God
That his blessings are to be shared

His love is boundless
And endless it goes
To show you the rhythm
Of life in it's flow

Never Give Up

When you think that you're alone
And don't know where to turn
Know that God is watching
So your candle will always burn

So try a little harder
And be sure that you will see
God's outpouring of splendour
Blessings of love, without a fee

Push Through

When you feel sadness and suffering
You must always push right through
'Cause everyone and anyone
Can sometimes feel sad and blue

God knows of your journey
He's with you every day
So Push straight through the darkness
And let God light you on your way